PLOT TWIST: I'M DEAD

An End-of-Life Planner for Authors

By Cara Bristol

Plot Twist: I'm Dead does not offer legal advice and should not be considered a legally binding document. Consult with an attorney for legal advice.

PLOT TWIST: I'M DEAD, AN END-OF-LIFE PLANNER FOR AUTHORS

ISBN: 978-1-970591-01-9

Edited by: Celeste Jones

Book cover design by: Sweet 'N Spicy Designs

Book formatting by: Sweet 'N Spicy Designs

Table of Contents

Why an End-of-Life Planner Just for Authors?

I recognized the need for an end-of-life planning workbook geared for authors after my mom passed in September 2024. I was executor of her estate and settling her affairs was easy. She'd made good arrangements, and she'd always been open with me about her financial matters, but most significantly, she was *old-school.* All her documents and accounts were on paper. She didn't do anything online.

I realized then my husband would be lost if something happened to me. Like many authors, I have royalties coming in from a myriad of sources at different times. I have scores of online accounts. If I died, deposits would magically appear in the checking account—until they didn't, but the bills and charges on the credit card would continue. My husband would have no idea who to contact to stop them. He wouldn't know how to get the year-end 1099s for taxes—or even that he *needed* to get them. Income would go unreported. He'd have no idea where to find expense receipts. Worse, if we both got hit by a bus at the same time, our out-of-state daughter would have even less of a clue what to do.

Settling my mom's estate served as the impetus to start documenting the details of my author life and preparing instructions for my husband.

I looked at other "end of life" organizers, which, while helpful for the usual household matters, did not serve the specific needs of writers. I couldn't find a single appropriate planner.

So, I wrote one.

Plot Twist: I'm Dead doesn't address estate planning or funeral arrangements. It focuses strictly on publishing matters and organizes the information your *book manager designee* will need to know in the event of your death—or your hospitalization or temporary/permanent incapacitation. You don't need to be dead to benefit from this book. Lol.

If you were unable to write for an extended period of time, who would manage your publishing business? Would that person have the necessary information to access your accounts? This planner is useful for that scenario, too.

Please note *Plot Twist* is not a legally binding document, but a source of information and instructions for whoever will inherit/manage your intellectual property. Consult with an attorney to name a legal designee.

How to Use This Planner

Author needs will vary. Some writers self-publish, others have a publisher, and hybrids do both. Some indies are "wide" and publish with multiple booksellers; others put their books in Kindle Unlimited and only publish on Amazon. There are ebooks, paperbacks, hardbacks, audiobooks, and foreign translations. Some writers use multiple pen names; others go by their legal name. I tried to address as many scenarios as I could think of. If a section in this workbook doesn't apply to you, skip it—although I recommend writing 'not applicable' on the page to avoid any uncertainty.

Getting the most out of this end-of-life planner will require you to make some key decisions (it's a *planner*), which I'll get to in a moment. Before I do, I'd like to highlight a few key sections.

"First Things First" will be a significant help for whoever manages your literary estate. When completed, this workbook will contain a mountain of information. Unfamiliar with publishing, your book manager may not know what's important or how to begin to settle your book affairs. Use First Things First to spell out the highest priority tasks and make it easier on him or her to carry out your wishes.

Fill out First Things First ***AFTER*** *you have completed the other workbook sections.* Completing the data pages first will help you to define what you want done ASAP and what can wait.

My hope is that as you fill in the data, you will begin to define and decide what you want done with your intellectual property estate overall—if you haven't thought about it already.

Another critical section is "Intellectual Property Management." This is where major decisions come into play. You'll need to decide *who* you want to manage your backlist and/or inherit the copyright to your works. This is something that needs to be done *legally*, not just designated in this workbook.

"Wishes for Your Published Books" is also important. When you're gone, your book manager/copyright owner will have a lot of leeway. What do you want him or her to do with your books? "Let them ride," i.e. take no action, and allow royalties to dwindle to nothing? Or is it your intention for your backlist to provide a continuous income stream for your beneficiary? This is something you should discuss with your designee as it will influence what accounts get closed, and which ones remain active.

If you need more space for instructions, you'll find note pages throughout.

There are sections for you to write a final message to your readers and fans. If you find writing long-hand laborious like I do and/or you need more space, you may choose to write your message on the computer and then attach a printout to the appropriate page or *give very clear instructions* on how to access the message document file.

Filling out the planner may seem daunting, but if you tackle it a little bit at a time, you'll have a complete set of instructions faster than you think. Keep *Plot Twist* handy, and when you login to book-related sites, jot the information in the planner. A little tip: use pencil for passwords and other information that may change.

Lastly, it probably goes without saying, but I'll say it anyway—keep the completed workbook in a secure place and inform the person who will be using it that it exists and where to find it.

Important Basic Facts

Date this document was completed: ______________________________

Full legal name: ______________________________

Date of birth: ______________ Place of birth ______________

Social Security Number______________________________

Address______________________________

Email ______________ Phone______________

How published? □ Traditional □ Indie/Self-Published □ Hybrid (Trad & Indie)

Pen name ______________________________

Email______________ Password______________

Pen name ______________________________

Email______________ Password______________

Pen name ______________________________

Email______________ Password______________

Other email used: ______________ Password______________

Other email used: ______________ Password______________

Other email used: ______________ Password______________

Other emails used: ______________________________

Other emails used: ______________________________

Other emails used: ______________________________

Pen name mailing address: ______________________________

Author website URL*______________________________

Author website URL*______________________________

Author website URL*______________________________

Author website URL*______________________________

*There is a separate section for website login and hosting information.

Basic Information Notes

Use this space to record additional emails, pen names, websites, etc.

Electronics

List the electronic devices you use in your writing and publishing career. Give a description of the item (laptop, desktop, tablet) and logins. Note: cell phone information is important because some accounts/websites require two-factor authentication.

Wi-Fi password: ______________________________

Device: ______________________ Login/PIN ______________________

Device: ______________________ Login/PIN ______________________

Device: ______________________ Login/PIN ______________________

Device: ______________________ Login/PIN ______________________

Device: ______________________ Login/PIN ______________________

Phone type: ______________ Number ______________ PIN ______________

Notes: ______________________________

First Things First—What to Do ASAP

What does your book manager need to do right away? Are there key people who should be contacted? Do ads need to be canceled? Are there monthly charges that should be stopped immediately? Fill out this section after you've completed the rest of the workbook.

Later Do This

Notification Contact List

Who should be notified of your passing, e.g., friends, co-authors, your agent, cover designers, editors, proofreaders, beta readers, personal assistant, publicist, the head of your fan club, etc.?

Name	Function	Email	Phone

Name	Function	Email	Phone

Intellectual Property Management

The most important decision(s) you'll make is who inherits the copyright to your books and manages your backlist and works-in-progress. (Mostly likely, this will be the same person, but it could be two separate individuals). ***Be sure to discuss your intentions with the prospective individual*** *to ensure he or she feels capable of handling the task—and wishes to do so. You can't assume someone will be as interested in preserving your legacy as you are. Once you have settled on an appropriate person, you must finalize the designation legally, i.e. name the person in your will. Always keep in mind, this planner is not a legally-binding document but rather a set of how-to instructions for the person legally designated to manage your backlist and/or inherit the copyright to your books.*

Do you have a will: □ Yes □ No

Location of the will: ______________________________

Name of attorney who prepared your will: ______________________________

His/her law firm: ______________________________

Address: ______________________________

Phone: ____________________ Email____________________

Does your will state who inherits the copyright/ownership of your books/intellectual property?

□ Yes □ No

Who is granted the copyright/legal ownership of your books?

Beneficiary's name: ______________________________

Address: ______________________________

Phone: ____________________ Email____________________

Is the legal copyright owner designee the one who will manage your backlist:

□ Yes □ No

If you have a separate intellectual property *manager* designated, list that person's info here:

Manager's name: ______________________________

Address: ______________________________

Phone: ______________________________Email______________________________

Are your books *registered* with the U.S. Copyright Office? (If some, but not all, note which ones in the Book Title section.)

□ All of them □ Some of them □ None of them

Location of the copyright forms: ______________________________

Note: Use https://www.login.gov/ to login to the U.S. Copyright Office.

Email: ______________________________Password______________________________

Cell phone/cell pin (to receive the authentication code) ______________________________

Notes

____

____

____

____

Royalties

List the book vendors and or publishers that send you royalties. There are separate sections to provide more information on each vendor/publisher and financial institutions.

Vendor or publisher	Payment frequency	Where the money is deposited

Vendor or publisher	Payment frequency	Where the money is deposited

Vendor or publisher	Payment frequency	Where the money is deposited

Notes

Book Vendor Contact Information

If you are self-published, list the vendors (Amazon, Barnes & Noble Press, Apple, Smashwords, Ingram, Audible, etc.) where your books are sold. If you're traditionally published, skip to the section on book publishers. "Author dashboard URL" is the vendor website page where you login to manage your book listings. Ex: for Amazon, it would be https://kdp.amazon.com/

Vendor: ______________________________

Author dashboard URL: ______________________________

Login name/email: ____________________ Password____________________

Notes: ______________________________

Vendor: ______________________________

Author dashboard URL: ______________________________

Login name/email: ____________________ Password____________________

Notes: ______________________________

Vendor: ______________________________

Author dashboard URL: ______________________________

Login name/email: ____________________ Password____________________

Notes: ______________________________

Vendor: ______________________________

Author dashboard URL: ______________________________

Login name/email: ______________________Password______________

Notes: ______________________________

Vendor: ______________________________

Author dashboard URL: ______________________________

Login name/email: ______________________Password______________

Notes: ______________________________

Vendor: ______________________________

Author dashboard URL: ______________________________

Login name/email: ______________________Password______________

Notes: ______________________________

Vendor: ____

Author dashboard URL: ______________________________________

Login name/email: ______________________ Password______________

Notes: ____

Vendor: ____

Author dashboard URL: ______________________________________

Login name/email: ______________________ Password______________

Notes: ____

Vendor: ____

Author dashboard URL: ______________________________________

Login name/email: ______________________ Password______________

Notes: ____

Vendor: ____

Author dashboard URL: ____

Login name/email: ______________________Password_____________

Notes: ____

Vendor: ____

Author dashboard URL: ____

Login name/email: ______________________Password_____________

Notes: ____

Vendor: ____

Author dashboard URL: ____

Login name/email: ______________________Password_____________

Notes: ____

Vendor: ____

Author dashboard URL: ____________________________________

Login name/email: ______________________Password____________

Notes: ____

Vendor: ____

Author dashboard URL: ____________________________________

Login name/email: ______________________Password____________

Notes: ____

Vendor: ____

Author dashboard URL: ____________________________________

Login name/email: ______________________Password____________

Notes: ____

Literary Agents

Does your agent represent all your books or just some of them? Do you have more than one agent? Give clear instructions where to find your agenting contract. You may wish to note the contract expiration date and the percentage your agent receives.

Do you have an agent? □ Yes □ No

Agency: ______________________________

Agent's name: ______________________________

Email: ____________________ Phone____________________

Mailing address: ______________________________

Contract location: ______________________________

Book projects represented and other notes: ______________________________

____

____

____

____

____

____

____

Agency: ______________________________

Agent's name: ______________________________

Email: ____________________ Phone ____________________

Mailing address: ______________________________

Contract location: ______________________________

Book projects represented and other notes: ______________________________

____

____

____

____

____

____

____

____

____

____

Agency: ____

Agent's name: ____

Email: ______________________ Phone ______________________

Mailing address: ____

Contract location: ____

Book projects represented and other notes: ______________________

____

____

____

____

____

____

____

____

____

____

More Notes

Book Publishers

If you're traditionally published or a hybrid, list the contact information for your publishers. See also the Book Titles section, where you can list your books and their respective publishers.

Publisher: ____________________

Contact person: ____________________

Email: ____________________ Phone ____________________

Mailing address: ____________________

Publishing contract location: ____________________

Notes: ____________________

____

Publisher: ____________________

Contact person: ____________________

Email: ____________________ Phone ____________________

Mailing address: ____________________

Publishing contract location: ____________________

Notes: ____________________

____

Publisher: ______________________________

Contact person: ______________________________

Email: ____________________ Phone ____________________

Mailing address: ______________________________

Publishing contract location: ______________________________

Notes: ______________________________

____

Publisher: ______________________________

Contact person: ______________________________

Email: ____________________ Phone ____________________

Mailing address: ______________________________

Publishing contract location: ______________________________

Notes: ______________________________

____

Publisher: ____

Contact person: ____

Email: ______________________ Phone ____________________

Mailing address: _______________________________________

Publishing contract location: _____________________________

Notes: ____

____

Publisher: ____

Contact person: ____

Email: ______________________ Phone ____________________

Mailing address: _______________________________________

Publishing contract location: _____________________________

Notes: ____

____

Financial Institution Information—Banks

Financial institution: ____

Name under which the account is held: ___________________________________

App on phone? ☐ Yes ☐ No

Account number: _________________________ Routing number ____________

Website URL ____

Login: ______________________________ Password __________________

Security questions/answers: ____

____

____

____

____

____

Address: ____

Phone: ____

Financial institution: ______________________________

Name under which the account is held: ______________________________

App on phone? □ Yes □ No

Account number: ______________________________ Routing number ________________

Website URL ______________________________

Login: ______________________________ Password ________________

Security questions/answers: ______________________________

____

____

____

____

____

Address: ______________________________

Phone: ______________________________

Financial Institution Info—Online Payment Services

Use this section for services like PayPal and Venmo.

Service: ____

App on phone? □ Yes □ No

Login: ______________________________ Password ____________________

Service: ____

App on phone? □ Yes □ No

Login: ______________________________ Password ____________________

Service: ____

App on phone? □ Yes □ No

Login: ______________________________ Password ____________________

Service: ____

App on phone? □ Yes □ No

Login: ______________________________ Password ____________________

Credit Cards

Credit card type (Visa, Mastercard, etc.): ______________________________

Name on the card: ______________________________

Account number: ______________________________

Expiration date ____________ CVC ____________

Member services phone: ______________ Call-in PIN ____________

Credit card type (Visa, Mastercard, etc.): ______________________________

Name on the card: ______________________________

Account number: ______________________________

Expiration date ____________ CVC ____________

Member services phone: ______________ Call-in PIN ____________

Credit card type (Visa, Mastercard, etc.): ______________________________

Name on the card: ______________________________

Account number: ______________________________

Expiration date ____________ CVC ____________

Member services phone: ______________ Call-in PIN ____________

Credit card type (Visa, Mastercard, etc.): ______________________________

Name on the card: ______________________________

Account number: ______________________________

Expiration date______________CVC______________

Member services phone: ______________Call-in PIN______________

Credit card type (Visa, Mastercard, etc.): ______________________________

Name on the card: ______________________________

Account number: ______________________________

Expiration date______________CVC______________

Member services phone: ______________Call-in PIN______________

Credit card type (Visa, Mastercard, etc.): ______________________________

Name on the card: ______________________________

Account number: ______________________________

Expiration date______________CVC______________

Member services phone: ______________Call-in PIN______________

Financial Institution Notes

Outgo—Author Expenses and Bills

Record recurring expenses (don't forget the annual ones!), e.g., newsletter service provider, graphics sites, and website hosting fee. List how often the fee is paid under frequency, and how you are charged (credit card, PayPal, automatic deduction from a bank account) under how billed. Under instructions you can state whether you wish to have the account canceled or have it continue. Advertising and royalties you pay to co-authors are separate sections.

Site: ________________________________ URL ________________________________

Login: ______________________________ Password ______________________________

Fee amount: ____________ Frequency: ______________ How billed: ___________________

What the site is used for: ____

Instructions: ____

Site: ________________________________ URL ________________________________

Login: ______________________________ Password ______________________________

Fee amount: ____________ Frequency: ______________ How billed: ___________________

What the site is used for: ____

Instructions: ____

Site: ______________________________ URL ______________________________

Login: ______________________________ Password ______________________________

Fee amount: ____________ Frequency: ______________ How billed: __________________

What the site is used for: ____

Instructions: ____

Site: ______________________________ URL ______________________________

Login: ______________________________ Password ______________________________

Fee amount: ____________ Frequency: ______________ How billed: __________________

What the site is used for: ____

Instructions: ____

Site: ______________________________ URL ______________________________

Login: ______________________________ Password ______________________________

Fee amount: ____________ Frequency: ______________ How billed: __________________

What the site is used for: ____

Instructions: ____

Site: ______________________________ URL ______________________________

Login: ______________________________ Password ______________________________

Fee amount: ____________ Frequency: ______________ How billed: __________________

What the site is used for: ____

Instructions: ____

Site: ______________________________ URL ______________________________

Login: ______________________________ Password ______________________________

Fee amount: ____________ Frequency: ______________ How billed: __________________

What the site is used for: ____

Instructions: ____

Site: ______________________________ URL ______________________________

Login: ______________________________ Password ______________________________

Fee amount: ____________ Frequency: ______________ How billed: __________________

What the site is used for: ____

Instructions: ____

Site: ______________________________ URL ______________________________

Login: ______________________________ Password ______________________________

Fee amount: ____________ Frequency: ______________ How billed: __________________

What the site is used for: ____

Instructions: ____

Site: ______________________________ URL ______________________________

Login: ______________________________ Password ______________________________

Fee amount: ____________ Frequency: ______________ How billed: __________________

What the site is used for: ____

Instructions: ____

Site: ______________________________ URL ______________________________

Login: ______________________________ Password ______________________________

Fee amount: ____________ Frequency: ______________ How billed: __________________

What the site is used for: ____

Instructions: ____

Site: ________________________________ URL ________________________________

Login: ______________________________ Password ______________________________

Fee amount: ____________ Frequency: ______________ How billed: __________________

What the site is used for: ____

Instructions: ____

Site: ________________________________ URL ________________________________

Login: ______________________________ Password ______________________________

Fee amount: ____________ Frequency: ______________ How billed: __________________

What the site is used for: ____

Instructions: ____

Site: ________________________________ URL ________________________________

Login: ______________________________ Password ______________________________

Fee amount: ____________ Frequency: ______________ How billed: __________________

What the site is used for: ____

Instructions: ____

Site: ______________________________ URL________________________________

Login: ____________________________ Password_____________________________

Fee amount: ___________ Frequency: _____________ How billed: __________________

What the site is used for: ____

Instructions: ____

Site: ______________________________ URL________________________________

Login: ____________________________ Password_____________________________

Fee amount: ___________ Frequency: _____________ How billed: __________________

What the site is used for: ____

Instructions: ____

Site: ______________________________ URL________________________________

Login: ____________________________ Password_____________________________

Fee amount: ___________ Frequency: _____________ How billed: __________________

What the site is used for: ____

Instructions: ____

Expense Notes

Outgo—Royalties You Pay to Other Authors

If you co-author ***and are responsible for paying your writing partner his/her share of the royalties****, list those "expenses" here. If you* ***receive*** *royalties from a co-author, record the payments in the Royalties section.* ***Important****: also fill out the section on co-authors.*

Co-author legal name____

Pen name____

Books/projects____

Books/projects____

Books/projects____

Co-author mailing address ____

____

Email ______________________________ Phone______________________

Frequency paid (monthly, quarterly, etc.) ________________________________

Payment method (e.g. PayPal, Venmo, mailing a check). Include any necessary information, such as a PayPal email, account numbers, etc. ________________________________

____

____

Co-author legal name____

Pen name____

Books/projects____

Books/projects____

Books/projects____

Co-author mailing address ____

____

Email ______________________________Phone________________________

Frequency paid (monthly, quarterly, etc)________________________________

Payment method (e.g., PayPal, Venmo, mailing a check). Include any necessary information, such as a PayPal email, account numbers, etc.: ________________________________

____

____

Co-Author Expense Notes

Advertising

Some authors advertise continuously. Some only advertise intermittently, and some not at all. If there's a possibility *you **might** have ads running, list them here. You probably would not want to have a Facebook or Amazon ad with no end date running at the time of your death.*

Advertiser: ______________________________ Dashboard URL: __________________________

Login: __________________________________ Password: ______________________________

Advertiser: ______________________________ Dashboard URL: __________________________

Login: __________________________________ Password: ______________________________

Advertiser: ______________________________ Dashboard URL: __________________________

Login: __________________________________ Password: ______________________________

Advertiser: ______________________________ Dashboard URL: __________________________

Login: __________________________________ Password: ______________________________

Advertiser: ______________________________ Dashboard URL: __________________________

Login: __________________________________ Password: ______________________________

Advertising Notes

Author Websites

What do you want to do with your website (s)? Keep it temporarily, maintain it permanently, or take it down? If you sell books or other merchandise on the site, what do you want to do about that? Selling books refers to ***direct*** *sales, not sales on vendors like Amazon or Barnes & Noble.*

Website URL: ____

Do you do *direct* book sales on this website: □ Yes □ No

Do you sell other merchandise on this website? □ Yes □ No

Website dashboard URL:____

Dashboard login: ______________________Password__________________

Website hosted at: ____________________URL: ____________________

Host site login: ______________________ Password: ________________

Other host info: ____

Domain name with: ___________________URL_____________________

Login: ___________________________Password: __________________

Other domain name info: ______________________________________

Website designer/manager_______________________________________

Web designer contact info: _____________________________________

____

What do you want to happen to this website? Keep it up or take it down? If you sell books or merchandise, you'll need to give instructions for that, too.

Website URL: ____

Do you sell books off this website: ☐ Yes ☐ No

Do you sell other merchandise on this website? ☐ Yes ☐ No

Website dashboard URL:____

Dashboard login: ________________________Password____________________

Website hosted at: ______________________URL: ______________________

Host site login: ________________________ Password: __________________

Other host info: ____

Domain name with: _____________________URL_______________________

Login: _______________________________Password: __________________

Other domain name info: ____

Website designer/manager____

Web designer contact info: ____

____

What do you want to happen to this website? Keep it up or take it down? If you sell books or merchandise, you'll need to give instructions for that, too.

Website URL: ______________________________

Do you sell books off this website: □ Yes □ No

Do you sell other merchandise on this website? □ Yes □ No

Website dashboard URL:______________________________

Dashboard login: ______________________________Password______________________________

Website hosted at: ______________________________URL: ______________________________

Host site login: ______________________________ Password: ______________________________

Other host info: ______________________________

Domain name with: ______________________________URL______________________________

Login: ______________________________Password: ______________________________

Other domain name info: ______________________________

Website designer/manager______________________________

Web designer contact info: ______________________________

____

What do you want to happen to this website? Keep it up or take it down? If you sell books or merchandise, you'll need to give instructions for that, too.

Author Newsletter

Do you want your newsletter service account deleted? Or do you want to keep it active so your book manager/inheritor can continue to email your subscribers? Do you wish to send out a final email to your subscribers? Do you have newsletter accounts that are inactive/paused that can be closed? You may wish to advise your book manager to download a spreadsheet of your subscribers BEFORE closing an active account just in case they later wish to reestablish the newsletter. Remember to record the service fee in the expense section.

Newsletter service provider____

Website URL____

Login/email________________________Password____________________

Other login info: ____

Address used for your newsletter____

____

Do you wish to email an announcement about your passing to your subscribers?

□ Yes □ No

What should be done about your account? □ Keep it open □ Close it

____

____

____

Final Email Message to Your Subscribers

Inactive Newsletter Service Accounts

If there is an inactive, but open account, you'll probably want to close it.

Newsletter service provider____

Website URL____

Login/email_________________________Password___________________

Other login info: ____

Address used for your newsletter_____________________________________

____

What should be done about your account? □ Keep it open □ Close it

Notes

____

____

____

____

____

____

____

Facebook

What should happen to your Facebook account/s? Do you want a memorialized profile where family, friends, and readers can share memories of you? Or do you want your profile deleted?

For a memorialized profile, you must ***designate a legacy contact on Facebook*** *to manage it. Naming that person here isn't enough. Facebook needs to know who it is. Two points of note: first, you must designate this contact on Facebook* ***before you die****. Second, the memorial only applies to your profile, not author pages.*

You don't need a designated legacy contact to have your account deleted, but the responsible person will need to provide proof of death and/or the authority to act on your behalf.

Go to the Facebook help page ***https://www.facebook.com/help/103897939701143****, for more complete instructions. If the aforementioned URL has changed, search for "report a death" in the Facebook Help and Support Center.*

What should happen to your **profile** account? □ Memorialize it □ Delete it

Legacy designee: ____

Contact info for designee: ____________________________________

Profile login email: ______________________ Password________________

Message to your readers to be posted on Facebook

____

____

____

____

____

____

Author Facebook Pages

Page name________________________________ □ Keep □ Delete

Page URL: ____

Page name________________________________ □ Keep □ Delete

Page URL: ____

Page name________________________________ □ Keep □ Delete

Page URL: ____

Page name________________________________ □ Keep □ Delete

Page URL: ____

Page name________________________________ □ Keep □ Delete

Page URL: ____

Page name________________________________ □ Keep □ Delete

Page URL: ____

Page name________________________________ □ Keep □ Delete

Page URL: ____

Page name________________________________ □ Keep □ Delete

Page URL: ____

Facebook Groups for Which You Are an Administrator

If there are other administrators in the group, you don't need to do anything, except add them to the notification list that you've passed. But if you're the sole admin, when Facebook learns of your death, the group will be paused, and Facebook will randomly contact members to see if they wish to assume the role. If no one does, the group will remain paused. You may decide to have someone delete the group before reporting your death.

Group name________________________________ □ Keep □ Delete

Group URL: ____

Group name________________________________ □ Keep □ Delete

Group URL: ____

Group name________________________________ □ Keep □ Delete

Group URL: ____

Group name________________________________ □ Keep □ Delete

Group URL: ____

Group name________________________________ □ Keep □ Delete

Group URL: ____

Group name________________________________ □ Keep □ Delete

Group URL: ____

Other Social Media Accounts

Site URL	Login	Password
Instructions:		
Instructions:		
Instructions:		
Instructions:		
Instructions:		
Instructions:		
Instructions		
Instructions:		
Instructions:		

Message to Readers to be Posted on Social Media

Miscellaneous Author Accounts

Use this section to list any other online accounts you wish to close or keep, e.g. Bowker, BookBub, free book promo sites. Accounts for which you pay a fee should also be listed under Outgo—Author Expenses and Bills.

Site URL	Login	Password
Instructions:		
Instructions:		
Instructions:		
Instructions:		
Instructions:		
Instructions:		
Instructions		
Instructions:		

Site URL	Login	Password
Instructions:		
Instructions:		
Instructions:		
Instructions:		
Instructions:		
Instructions:		
Instructions		
Instructions:		
Instructions:		
Instructions:		

Co-Authors and Ghostwriters

Do you write with a co-author or a ghostwriter? If you are responsible for sending the person his or her share of the royalties, complete the information under Outgo—Royalties You Pay to Other Authors. Use the notes section here to indicate how long your books will be listed, when/if the rights revert to you, and any agreements you've made with your co-author. Anthology info can be listed here or under Group Projects.

Name: ____

Email: ______________________ Phone: ________________

Mailing address: ______________________________________

Do you have a written contract: □ Yes □ No

Location of contract: __________________________________

Notes: ____

____

____

____

____

____

____

____

Name: ____

Email: ______________________ Phone: __________________

Do you have a written contract: ☐ Yes ☐ No

Location of contract: ____________________________________

Mailing address: ____

Notes: ____

____

____

____

____

____

____

____

____

____

____

____

Group Projects You're Involved In

Obviously, group projects change from month to month, year to year. But if there are any long-term ongoing projects, you should list them here, along with the person to notify OR the website login info. Examples might include an annual conference, an ongoing newsletter builder, an annual anthology you coordinate, or BookFunnel promotions you run all the time.

Project: ____

Contact (name and email): ______________________________

Website URL/login/password: ____________________________

Do you have a written contract: □ Yes □ No

Location of contract: __________________________________

Notes: ____

____

Project: ____

Contact (name and email): ______________________________

Website URL/login/password: ____________________________

Do you have a written contract: □ Yes □ No

Location of contract: __________________________________

Notes: ____

____

Project: ____

Contact (name and email): ______________________________________

Website URL/login/password: ______________________________________

Do you have a written contract: ☐ Yes ☐ No

Location of contract: ______________________________________

Notes: ____

____

Project: ____

Contact (name and email): ______________________________________

Website URL/login/password: ______________________________________

Do you have a written contract: ☐ Yes ☐ No

Location of contract: ______________________________________

Notes: ____

____

Project: ____

Contact (name and email): ___________________________

Website URL/login/password: _________________________

Do you have a written contract: □ Yes □ No

Location of contract: _______________________________

Notes: ____

____

Project: ____

Contact (name and email): ___________________________

Website URL/login/password: _________________________

Do you have a written contract: □ Yes □ No

Location of contract: _______________________________

Notes: ____

____

Professional Organizations

If you belong to any author organizations, list them here. Important note: be sure to give the name used to join the organization (legal name v. pen name). Record any dues you pay in the section on Outgo—Author Expenses and Bills.

Organization____

Your name _________________________________Membership number______________

Instructions: ____

Organization contact info (i.e. website & login, email, etc.): __________________________

____

Organization____

Your name _________________________________Membership number______________

Instructions: ____

Organization contact info (i.e. website & login, email, etc.): __________________________

____

Organization____

Your name ______________________________Membership number______________

Instructions: ____

Organization contact info (i.e. website & login, email, etc.): ______________________

____

Organization____

Your name ______________________________Membership number______________

Instructions: ____

Organization contact info (i.e. website & login, email, etc.): ______________________

____

Organization____

Your name ______________________________Membership number______________

Instructions: ____

Organization contact info (i.e. website & login, email, etc.): ______________________

____

Book Titles

This section will help your book manager/owner locate your books since you may use different publishers/vendors for different books or genres. There are 159 lines to record book titles. If you've been extremely prolific and have more titles, list the book series and number of books in the series, rather than individual titles. Use the book file location to help your designee find the manuscript. What is the file name? Where is it stored? In the cloud? On a disk? On your hard drive? List the formats the book is published in. Refer to the separate Book Publisher section to provide publisher contact and contract information.

Book Title or Series	Book File Location
Formats:	
Vendors or publisher:	
Formats:	
Vendors or publisher:	
Formats:	
Vendors or publisher:	
Formats:	
Vendors or publisher:	
Formats:	
Vendors or publisher:	

Book Title or Series	Book File Location
Formats:	
Vendors or publisher:	
Formats:	
Vendors or publisher:	
Formats:	
Vendors or publisher:	
Formats:	
Vendors or publisher:	
Formats:	
Vendors or publisher:	
Formats:	
Vendors or publisher:	
Formats:	
Vendors or publisher:	

Book Title or Series	Book File Location
Formats:	
Vendors or publisher:	
Formats:	
Vendors or publisher:	
Formats:	
Vendors or publisher:	
Formats:	
Vendors or publisher:	
Formats:	
Vendors or publisher:	
Formats:	
Vendors or publisher:	
Formats:	
Vendors or publisher:	

Book Title or Series	Book File Location
Formats:	
Vendors or publisher:	
Formats:	
Vendors or publisher:	
Formats:	
Vendors or publisher:	
Formats:	
Vendors or publisher:	
Formats:	
Vendors or publisher:	
Formats:	
Vendors or publisher:	
Formats:	
Vendors or publisher:	

Book Title or Series	Book File Location
Formats:	
Vendors or publisher:	
Formats:	
Vendors or publisher:	
Formats:	
Vendors or publisher:	
Formats:	
Vendors or publisher:	
Formats:	
Vendors or publisher:	
Formats:	
Vendors or publisher:	
Formats:	
Vendors or publisher:	

Book Title or Series	Book File Location
Formats:	
Vendors or publisher:	
Formats:	
Vendors or publisher:	
Formats:	
Vendors or publisher:	
Formats:	
Vendors or publisher:	
Formats:	
Vendors or publisher:	
Formats:	
Vendors or publisher:	
Formats:	
Vendors or publisher:	

Book Title or Series	Book File Location
Formats:	
Vendors or publisher:	
Formats:	
Vendors or publisher:	
Formats:	
Vendors or publisher:	
Formats:	
Vendors or publisher:	
Formats:	
Vendors or publisher:	
Formats:	
Vendors or publisher:	
Formats:	
Vendors or publisher:	

Book Title or Series	Book File Location
Formats:	
Vendors or publisher:	
Formats:	
Vendors or publisher:	
Formats:	
Vendors or publisher:	
Formats:	
Vendors or publisher:	
Formats:	
Vendors or publisher:	
Formats:	
Vendors or publisher:	
Formats:	
Vendors or publisher:	

Book Title or Series	Book File Location
Formats:	
Vendors or publisher:	
Formats:	
Vendors or publisher:	
Formats:	
Vendors or publisher:	
Formats:	
Vendors or publisher:	
Formats:	
Vendors or publisher:	
Formats:	
Vendors or publisher:	
Formats:	
Vendors or publisher:	

Book Title or Series	Book File Location
Formats:	
Vendors or publisher:	
Formats:	
Vendors or publisher:	
Formats:	
Vendors or publisher:	
Formats:	
Vendors or publisher:	
Formats:	
Vendors or publisher:	
Formats:	
Vendors or publisher:	
Formats:	
Vendors or publisher:	

Book Title or Series	Book File Location
Formats:	
Vendors or publisher:	
Formats:	
Vendors or publisher:	
Formats:	
Vendors or publisher:	
Formats:	
Vendors or publisher:	
Formats:	
Vendors or publisher:	
Formats:	
Vendors or publisher:	
Formats:	
Vendors or publisher:	

Book Title or Series	Book File Location
Formats:	
Vendors or publisher:	
Formats:	
Vendors or publisher:	
Formats:	
Vendors or publisher:	
Formats:	
Vendors or publisher:	
Formats:	
Vendors or publisher:	
Formats:	
Vendors or publisher:	
Formats:	
Vendors or publisher:	

Book Title or Series	Book File Location
Formats:	
Vendors or publisher:	
Formats:	
Vendors or publisher:	
Formats:	
Vendors or publisher:	
Formats:	
Vendors or publisher:	
Formats:	
Vendors or publisher:	
Formats:	
Vendors or publisher:	
Formats:	
Vendors or publisher:	

Book Title or Series	Book File Location
Formats:	
Vendors or publisher:	
Formats:	
Vendors or publisher:	
Formats:	
Vendors or publisher:	
Formats:	
Vendors or publisher:	
Formats:	
Vendors or publisher:	
Formats:	
Vendors or publisher:	
Formats:	
Vendors or publisher:	

Book Title or Series	**Book File Location**
Formats:	
Vendors or publisher:	
Formats:	
Vendors or publisher:	
Formats:	
Vendors or publisher:	
Formats:	
Vendors or publisher:	
Formats:	
Vendors or publisher:	
Formats:	
Vendors or publisher:	
Formats:	
Vendors or publisher:	

Book Title or Series	Book File Location
Formats:	
Vendors or publisher:	
Formats:	
Vendors or publisher:	
Formats:	
Vendors or publisher:	
Formats:	
Vendors or publisher:	
Formats:	
Vendors or publisher:	
Formats:	
Vendors or publisher:	
Formats:	
Vendors or publisher:	

Book Title or Series	Book File Location
Formats:	
Vendors or publisher:	
Formats:	
Vendors or publisher:	
Formats:	
Vendors or publisher:	
Formats:	
Vendors or publisher:	
Formats:	
Vendors or publisher:	
Formats:	
Vendors or publisher:	
Formats:	
Vendors or publisher:	

Book Title or Series	Book File Location
Formats:	
Vendors or publisher:	
Formats:	
Vendors or publisher:	
Formats:	
Vendors or publisher:	
Formats:	
Vendors or publisher:	
Formats:	
Vendors or publisher:	
Formats:	
Vendors or publisher:	
Formats:	
Vendors or publisher:	

Book Title or Series	Book File Location
Formats:	
Vendors or publisher:	
Formats:	
Vendors or publisher:	
Formats:	
Vendors or publisher:	
Formats:	
Vendors or publisher:	
Formats:	
Vendors or publisher:	
Formats:	
Vendors or publisher:	
Formats:	
Vendors or publisher:	

Book Title or Series	Book File Location
Formats:	
Vendors or publisher:	
Formats:	
Vendors or publisher:	
Formats:	
Vendors or publisher:	
Formats:	
Vendors or publisher:	
Formats:	
Vendors or publisher:	
Formats:	
Vendors or publisher:	
Formats:	
Vendors or publisher:	

Book Title or Series	Book File Location
Formats:	
Vendors or publisher:	
Formats:	
Vendors or publisher:	
Formats:	
Vendors or publisher:	
Formats:	
Vendors or publisher:	
Formats:	
Vendors or publisher:	
Formats:	
Vendors or publisher:	
Formats:	
Vendors or publisher:	

Book Title or Series	**Book File Location**
Formats:	
Vendors or publisher:	
Formats:	
Vendors or publisher:	
Formats:	
Vendors or publisher:	
Formats:	
Vendors or publisher:	
Formats:	
Vendors or publisher:	
Formats:	
Vendors or publisher:	
Formats:	
Vendors or publisher:	

Book Title or Series	Book File Location
Formats:	
Vendors or publisher:	
Formats:	
Vendors or publisher:	
Formats:	
Vendors or publisher:	
Formats:	
Vendors or publisher:	
Formats:	
Vendors or publisher:	
Formats:	
Vendors or publisher:	
Formats:	
Vendors or publisher:	

Your Wishes for Your Published Books

What should your loved ones/backlist manager do with your books?

Your Wishes for Works-in-Progress

At the time of your passing, you may have unfinished manuscripts. What is done with the manuscript will depend on how far along it is. Assuming you have drafts close to publication-ready, what should your book manager do with them?

Your Wishes for Out-of-Print Books

Maybe publishing rights reverted to you, or you had a novella in an anthology that you intended to rerelease as a single title. Should your book manager publish those works? Do the manuscripts require additional editing? Do they need new covers? Conversely, you might have old manuscripts sitting in your computer that you don't want published and wish to ensure they never see the light of day.

Negotiations and Disputes

Are you involved in any negotiations, contract disputes, or litigation with publishers, agents, or co-authors? Don't leave your book manager in the dark. Bring him or her up to speed here. Remember to include applicable contact information

Location of Important Documents

Where are your publishing-related documents physically located? On your hard drive? In the cloud? In a filing cabinet? Examples of things to include are publishing contracts, royalty spreadsheets, expense receipts/reports, copyright forms, LLC documents, and your will..

Document	Location

Document	Location

Document	Location

Do you have an account with DocuSign (or another similar service) that allows you to send and manage documents electronically? □ Yes □ No

Service________________________________URL______________________________

Login/password info____

Taxes, Taxes, Taxes

Tax preparer name: ______________________________

Email: ____________________ Phone: ____________________

Address: ______________________________

Location of past tax returns: ______________________________

Location of current expense receipts: ______________________________

1099s

Vendor/Publisher	How you get the 1099s (email, regular mail)	Login Info (if online)

Royalties for Which You Do Not Receive a 1099

You may receive royalties from foreign publishers, a co-author, the organizer of an anthology, or may not meet the minimum income threshold to receive a 1099. How can your book manager find/account for the income?

Company Name	Royalty Record Location (bank statement, spreadsheet on the hard drive, etc.)

Notes on Filing Income Taxes

Your Final Words, Notes, Instructions

About the Planner Author

Author Cara Bristol has published more than seventy-five books, mostly science fiction romance, but also two other nonfiction books—a sex scene thesaurus, *Naughty Words for Nice Writers*, and a humorous memoir, *You're Not Ugly to Look At.* She is the finance manager of her household and the keeper of the documents and was executor of her mother's estate. For information about the author, go to www.carabristol.com.

Acknowledgments

I knew as I was developing and writing this planner that I would need to get feedback from other authors. I want to give a huge shoutout and thanks to long-time author friends, Veronica Scott and Sue Lyndon, who provided invaluable suggestions. Likewise, I want to thank my friend and editor on the project, author Celeste Jones, for her fantastic suggestions and sharp eyes. Last, but not least, I give a big thanks to Jaycee DeLorenzo of Sweet 'N Spicy Designs who did the cover and formatting.

Glossary

Author dashboard/dashboard – the page on a website where authors control/manage their account.

Beta reader – a person provides feedback to the author on a manuscript before it is professionally edited and published. Not to be confused with an editor, a paid professional, who corrects errors and improves the writing/story-telling.

Copyright – the exclusive legal right to control how original literary works are used and distributed. A work is copyrighted once it is fixed in a tangible form such as being written down or saved to a computer. It does not need to be registered to be copyrighted, but registering a work affords the copyright owner additional legal protection.

Facebook Group – A place for people with shared interests to connect and talk about their interests. Author fan groups are Facebook groups.

Facebook Profile – A personal account on Facebook intended for individuals to share content with "friends." Many authors use their personal accounts to promote their books, but they also may have a Facebook Page (s).

Facebook Page – A commercial account for businesses or public figures to reach a public audience and/or advertise to that audience. Pages have "followers" instead of "friends." Many authors have an "Author Page" in addition to, or instead of, a profile.

Hybrid – An author who has books that are traditionally published and self-published.

Indie, independent publishing – Self-published.

Intellectual property (IP) – things created by a person's imagination that are protected by law such as artwork, books, or images. Literary works are protected by copyright.

KDP – Kindle Direct Publishing.

Kindle Direct Publishing – Amazon's self-publishing platform.

Kindle Select – An Amazon program allowing authors to enroll their ebooks in Kindle Unlimited in exchange for exclusivity. If an author's books are in Kindle Select/Kindle Unlimited, he or she cannot publish his or her ***ebooks*** anywhere else. (This does not apply to paperbacks, hardbacks or audiobooks). Kindle Select contracts are for ninety days and renew automatically. An author must manually cancel the renewal.

Kindle Unlimited – Amazon's subscription program for readers allowing them to borrow books for a monthly fee.

Literary agent – A professional who represents the author's interests in negotiations between the author and the publishing house for which the agent receives a percentage of the royalties paid to the author.

Royalty – A percentage of the income from the sale of a book paid to the author. Royalties are set by the contract with the publisher/publishing platform, and are paid on a regular schedule such as quarterly, bi-monthly, semi-annually.

Self-publishing – When authors publish their own books rather than go through an established publishing company.

Trad, traditionally published – Being published by a publishing company.

URL – A website address. Ex: www.carabristol.com. URL stands for Uniform Resource Locator.

Vendor – As used in *Plot Twist: I'm Dead*, vendor refers to the publishing platform or bookseller, e.g. Amazon, Apple books, Barnes & Noble, Audible, etc.

Wide – An author is "wide" if his or her books are available at multiple booksellers. (Some Indie authors publish only on Amazon).

Made in United States
North Haven, CT
05 November 2026